STEWARDED

Responsibility, Judgment, and the Discipline of the Long View

The Discipline of Stewardship in
Leadership, Capital, and Life

Charles Ho

Stewardship is practiced before outcomes are known.

Charles Ho
2800 W Parker Rd Ste 110, Plano, TX 75[illegible]75
stewarded@abcderealty.com

ISBN: 978-1-972345-03-0 (hardcover), 978-[illegible]-972345-04-7 (paperback), 978-1-972345-05-4 (eBook).

Printed in the United States of America

Dedication

To my wife Betty,

the real hero of the family, who recognized potential long before results, and who continues to love, encourage, nurture, challenge, and hold me accountable for what truly matters.

To our children—Elizabeth, Aaron, and Derek,

thank you for your patience, your joy, and your grace with my imperfect schedule and persistent curiosity.

To the mentors who invested time, truth, and discipline into my life, and to those who trusted me before I felt ready.

Above all,

to God, whose grace, patience, and provision made stewardship possible long before success appeared.

Table of Contents

Foreword

by Tom Ziglar

I've had the privilege of knowing Charles Ho not only as a business leader but as a man who takes responsibility seriously.

My father, Zig Ziglar, often said that you can have everything in life you want if you help enough other people get what they want. Charles embodies that principle—not as a slogan, but as a way of life. His success has been shaped less by ambition than by discipline, faith, and an uncommon commitment to doing things the right way, even when it would have been easier to do otherwise.

What has always stood out to me about Charles is his way of thinking.

He doesn't rush decisions. He doesn't chase recognition. He evaluates opportunity through the lens of stewardship—asking not just whether this can be done, but whether it should be done, and who will be affected if it is. That mindset is rare, especially in environments where speed and scale are often rewarded more than judgment and restraint.

This book reflects that mindset clearly.

Stewarded is not a story about quick wins or overnight success. It is a thoughtful account of how character is formed through responsibility, how faith governs decision-making, and how leadership is expressed through consistency over time. Charles is transparent about both successes and setbacks, and he shares lessons learned not to impress, but to serve.

Faith plays a central role in Charles's life, not as a performance but as a foundation. It informs how he leads, partners, and measures success. That quiet integration of belief and behavior is one of the reasons I respect him so deeply.

For readers looking for guarantees or shortcuts, this may not be the book they expect. But for those who understand that lasting success is built deliberately—through values, relationships, and disciplined action—Stewarded offers clarity and encouragement.

It has been an honor to walk alongside Charles as a friend and witness his growth as a leader. The principles shared in these pages will resonate with those who value integrity, faith, and long-term thinking.

— Tom Ziglar
CEO, Ziglar, Inc.

INTRODUCTION

Stewardship is practiced before outcomes are known.

Long before results can be measured, decisions are made—often quietly, often without recognition. These decisions reveal how responsibility is understood and how trust is handled when others are affected.

This book is not a record of success.

It is an explanation of judgment.

It is about how choices are made when information is incomplete, incentives are misaligned, and pressure favors speed over thoughtfulness. It is about restraint when action would be easier, and patience when urgency would be rewarded.

Stewardship does not announce itself. It shows up in preparation, in systems built to endure stress, and in decisions that protect people and capital even when no one is watching.

The stories that follow are not presented to persuade or impress. They are offered to provide transparency into how judgment was formed—through responsibility, failure, faith, and discipline—long before outcomes were visible.

If you are looking for guarantees, this book will disappoint.

If you are seeking clarity around how responsibility is carried, it may resonate.

The lessons in these pages were not formed in theory.

They were shaped through decades of operating businesses, managing capital, navigating partnerships, and carrying responsibility for outcomes that affected other people's lives.

The principles that follow were not designed for speed.

They were learned under pressure, refined through mistakes, and tested over time.

AUTHOR'S NOTE

This book was not written to explain success.

It was written to reflect on responsibility.

Over the course of my life, I have worked in many roles—son, immigrant, employee, entrepreneur, investor, husband, and father. Each role carried expectations, risks, and decisions whose consequences extended beyond me.

Looking back, the most important lessons were not about speed, ambition, or achievement. They were about judgment—how responsibility is carried when outcomes remain uncertain.

Many opportunities I encountered appeared attractive on the surface. Some were pursued. Others were intentionally declined. The difference was rarely visible in the moment. It became clear only with time.

The idea of stewardship gradually emerged as the framework that explained those decisions. Opportunity is rarely owned in the way we imagine. It is entrusted. The task is not merely to pursue outcomes, but to carry responsibility faithfully while outcomes unfold.

The chapters that follow describe moments that shaped that understanding. Some involve success. Others involve mistakes, restraint, or circumstances beyond control. Together they form the path through which the idea of stewardship became clear.

This book is not intended as instruction. It is a reflection on how responsibility, judgment, and patience shape a life over time.

HOW TO READ THIS BOOK

This book combines story and reflection.

Each chapter describes experiences that shaped my understanding of responsibility, judgment, and stewardship over time. The events are presented not as instructions, but as moments that clarified how leadership and responsibility are carried in practice.

At the end of each chapter, you will find a short lesson. These lessons summarize the principle that emerged from the experience described in the chapter.

The chapters follow the progression of a life shaped by responsibility:

- formation through work and adversity
- judgment developed through experience
- stewardship practiced through leadership
- continuity established through others

Some readers will prefer to read the book straight through. Others may return to individual chapters when facing similar decisions.

The goal of the book is not to prescribe formulas, but to reflect on how responsibility, discipline, and patience shape outcomes over time.

Stewardship rarely appears dramatic in the moment. It reveals itself slowly through decisions repeated consistently over years.

CHAPTER 1

Childhood and Work Ethic

> *Early responsibility teaches us how to recognize opportunity when it appears.*

My father placed several receipt books on the table and smirked.

"Three days," he said.

My father had left home at sixteen and never returned because of the Japanese invasion and the rise of communism in China. To the best of my knowledge, he carried multiple visible shrapnel wounds and served as a military intelligence officer.

Challenges were his method. He did not explain. He tested.

I was ten years old and wanted an Apple II computer. I wanted to play video games and learn programming like the kids I read about in magazines. My father agreed—under one condition. If I wanted the computer, I had three days to collect the money from newspaper customers myself.

At the time, I didn't realize what he was teaching me. I only knew I wanted that computer badly enough to try.

I was born in Taiwan when the United States was embroiled in the Vietnam War.

Shortly before my father retired from the military, he became an entrepreneur, delivering newspapers independently. After he was honorably discharged, he operated a stationery and loose tea retail store along with an advertising business.

My mother carried her own story of perseverance. She married young to escape a difficult rural farming life and learned early to bear responsibility beyond her years. Together, my parents built a life defined by work, sacrifice, and a simple belief: opportunity is created, not waited for.

My parents' work schedule meant continual work with one exception: the Chinese Lunar New Year, when newspaper printing presses rested for three days.

Morning paper deliveries ran from 4:00 a.m. to 7:30 a.m. Evening paper deliveries from 1:00 p.m. to 4:00 p.m. Then from 5:00 p.m. to 7:30 p.m., classifieds and advertisements were delivered to publishers for the next day's printing.

In addition, they maintained a storefront selling newspapers, magazines, periodicals, loose tea by weight, and stationery. I was raised in that store as far back as I can remember.

The store was small, but it was always busy.

My father and mother rotated picking up freshly printed bundles of newspapers from a central distribution point for all publications. They left in the dark around 4:30 a.m. By 5:00 a.m., they were back separating stacks and preparing them for delivery.

By 5:30 a.m., they were already moving through neighborhoods, depositing folded newspapers into mailboxes or tightly rolled copies thrown up to second- and third-story balconies. Occasionally a customer lowered a bucket on a rope from the fourth floor so the newspaper could be dropped inside.

All of this happened before sunrise seven days a week, 362 days a year.

By 7:30 a.m., they returned from deliveries and opened the store for retail customers who preferred to buy their newspapers in person. Some stayed only a moment. Others lingered, reading headlines while chatting with friends.

Before grade school, I spent hours watching the rhythm of the business.

In those days, most people paid with coins and small bills. I remember that the smallest coins were sometimes taped together in stacks to make counting faster during busy transactions.

When customers asked questions, my parents answered directly and without hurry. If a call came in about a missed or damaged delivery, they explained the situation honestly. There were no excuses—only explanations and solutions.

I did not realize it then, but I was observing how trust is built. Customers returned not simply because products were available, but because they trusted the people who provided them.

The store was not only a place of business. It was also where I learned how work, responsibility, and reputation were connected.

The challenge he gave me would test everything I had already learned.

I learned money handling and counting, selling, customer service, and logistics early. By the age of eight, I could ride public transit independently.

I started working in the family business, delivering advertisements to newspaper publishers. By age ten, I was selling newspapers, 2B pencils, and erasers outside unified examination centers.

The unified examination days were different.

Hundreds of students arrived early in the morning carrying books and notebooks. Parents waited outside, anxious and hopeful. For many families, those exams represented children's opportunity—entry into better schools and better futures.

I set up a small tarp near the entrance with a variety of supplies: newspapers, 2B pencils, erasers, pencil sharpeners, rulers, protractors, and compasses.

The pencils mattered more than anything else. If a student arrived without the correct pencil, they could not properly take the exam. That small detail created urgency. Many students realized their mistake only after arriving at the gate.

They rushed toward me.

I learned quickly that preparation mattered. If I ran out of pencils too early, I lost the sale—and more importantly, a student might struggle through the exam without the proper tools.

If I stocked too many, unsold inventory remained, and I had to haul it back to the family store.

By the end of the morning, most of whatever I brought would be sold.

Newspapers were often used by the waiting families for reading, spread on the grass for sitting, waved as a fan in the heat, or held overhead for shade. What I did not understand then was that I was learning the fundamentals of business: supply, demand, timing, and responsibility for outcomes.

If I failed to prepare, the sales opportunity was lost.

I assumed all parents worked like mine. To me, this was simply life.

Then the Apple II arrived.

The deadline forced urgency.

I started with newspaper routes where customers owed the largest balances and collected during dinner hours when they were most likely home.

When they told me to come back tomorrow, I returned the next evening — and the evening after that.

When they didn't pay, I showed up three consecutive nights.

My father did not celebrate the purchase. He simply nodded, as if the outcome had been expected all along. Only years later did I understand what that nod meant: the computer was never the point. The work was.

Long before I understood the word stewardship, I was already practicing it.

LESSON

Responsibility often appears before opportunity.

Stewardship begins when we accept the work required before the reward is visible.

CHAPTER 2

Immigration and Displacement

> *Displacement is not only geographic. It is the loss of the assumptions that once made the world understandable.*

Visitors to our store and family home often encouraged my parents to immigrate to countries in Central and South America such as Argentina, Brazil, Costa Rica, or Uruguay.

Their motivation was always the same: stability in case of war with China, better education, and greater opportunity for their children.

In preparation, my mother learned Portuguese. Later, she visited Costa Rica and the United States in 1981 and 1982.

By 1983, a decision was made.

Those final months in Taiwan felt different from ordinary life. Something had already shifted — in the way my parents spoke after the store closed at night, in the careful way my mother moved through familiar routines as though committing them to memory. A decision that large does not arrive cleanly. It settles in gradually, and then one morning it is simply true.

My father would stay behind with my older brother until his mandatory military service ended. My mother would take my younger sister and me to Los Angeles. The arrangement was described as temporary. In practice, we all understood, without saying so, that the family would never again live under the same roof in the same ordinary way. That understanding did not need to be spoken. It was simply present in the house, like the air.

The morning we left for the airport, my father stood at the door of the store. He did not say much. That was not his way. He had survived wars and displacement before I was born, and he had learned that composure was its own kind of protection. What I remember most is that he stood very still while everything around him was in motion — my mother managing luggage, my sister already moving toward the taxi, the street filling with its ordinary morning noise. He looked at me once, directly, and nodded. I understood it the same way I had understood his nod after the receipt books: that more was expected, and that he believed it would be delivered.

At fourteen, at the beginning of ninth grade, we left Taiwan for Los Angeles.

Until that moment, my world had been familiar. Overnight, everything required translation — language, culture, and expectations.

The flight itself was disorienting in ways I had not anticipated. Distance is abstract until it becomes hours of sky, and then arrival in a place where every sign, every announcement, every exchange between strangers is conducted in sounds you can parse but not yet assemble into meaning. Tokyo Narita International Airport. We had to exit and wait for transfer to the next flight.

The second flight was even longer than the first and I slept through most of the way. At the end of the second flight, we arrived at Los Angeles International Airport in the morning only a few hours from the time we left Taiwan. That was my first experience with the international date line, and I was fascinated by it.

The customs officer took a long time to process our paperwork and summoned an airline employee to help with our carry-on luggage and accompany us to the next flight. He stayed with us 'til we boarded.

I understood none of the announcements on the third flight and simply followed along. I had little recollection of that journey. Once the plane landed, passengers collected their belongings and headed to the front of the plane.

Mom grabbed my sister and me and said, "Leave everything and follow me."

We did.

From my mother's gestures to the flight attendant, I understood she was saying we were hungry. I never confirmed it, and it did not matter.

Mom took us straight to the airport exit and into a waiting taxi. In no more than 15 minutes we exited the taxi at a motel. Mom paid at the counter through a hole in the plexiglass and received a key on a big keychain. She took us to a room, and we fell to sleep almost immediately.

When I woke up, Mom was already on the motel phone in the room talking to someone in Chinese. Mom took us to a fast-food restaurant where I had my first hamburger meal in the U.S.

She then rushed us to the curb and hailed a taxi to Delta Airlines ticketing office in downtown Atlanta.

There a nice gentleman met us and helped us buy tickets to Los Angeles. Later, I learned that he was from the consulate helping stranded travelers.

Four flights in two calendar days. Taipei to Tokyo to Los Angeles to Atlanta to Los Angeles.

Mom checked us into a motel near Downtown Los Angeles. She left us at the motel and went to buy a rice cooker and some groceries. We survived by cooking rice, bacon, and vegetables in the rice cooker.

We stayed in the motel for a few days. Then my mother took us to a house where she rented two small rooms.

Thinking back, my room was roughly 50 square feet. Mom and my sister's room was about 100 square feet. We had the shared use of the bathroom and kitchen.

We were placed into schools — my sister attended a different one. Even simple instructions required an interpreter.

I remember the first week of school clearly. Not because dramatic things happened, but because the ordinary things were so completely unfamiliar that each one required its full share of attention.

The classroom was larger than the ones I had known in Taiwan, and louder, in a different way. Students in Taiwan sat in straight rows and faced the front. There was a formality to the arrangement that communicated expectations without a single word being said. Here the desks were grouped in clusters. Students turned to talk to each other while the teacher was still speaking. The noise had a different texture — more casual, more comfortable, built on a shared understanding of what was and was not permitted. I did not yet share that understanding.

None of my classmates spoke English. We were all learning. Most spoke Spanish.

My math book had English on one side and Spanish on the other. That was the first time I saw an upside-down question mark used at the beginning of the sentence.

The teacher spoke continuously, and the words came faster than I could separate them. I caught fragments — a number, a name, a direction — and assembled them into approximate meaning the way you might piece together a piece of paper after it went through a shredder or a broken sentence from its largest recognizable parts.

When I could not assemble enough pieces, I watched faces instead. I learned to read whether an answer was correct from the teacher's expression.

What I was learning in those first weeks was not language. It was attention.

LESSON

When familiar assumptions disappear, survival requires learning quickly and adjusting without complaint.

Adaptation is the decision to function before you feel ready.

CHAPTER 3

Adaptation and Competence

> *Competence is built before confidence arrives. The work comes first.*

The strategies that carried me through those first weeks in Los Angeles were not taught —they were discovered, one day at a time. I learned to identify the moment a lesson was ending from the shift in posture that preceded it. I learned that confusion looks the same in any language, and that confidence does too.

During the interactions with other students, I learned the phrase "papel y lapiz." (Paper and pencil in Spanish.)

When the teacher called on me, I answered with whatever vocabulary words I had — sometimes the right ones, sometimes close, sometimes entirely off. The other students' reactions told me which. Most were indifferent, the way students everywhere are indifferent to things that do not involve them. A few were kind. Occasionally someone would gesture quietly at the board or point to a page, offering guidance without making an event of it. Those small directions mattered more than the people offering them probably knew.

What I was learning in those first weeks was not language, at least not primarily. It was attention. I was developing a particular kind of watchfulness — the habit of gathering information from every available source because the most obvious source, the words themselves, was only partially available to me. That habit did not leave when the language finally came.

The school did not have a full-time interpreter. They pulled students out of other classes whenever necessary. I managed with expressions, gestures, and fragments of vocabulary. What I could not understand through words, I worked to understand through everything else.

High school in Los Angeles meant overcrowding and year-round schedules of four months on and two months off.

During school breaks I worked at a Chinese restaurant six days a week, from opening to closing. I started in the kitchen washing dishes and moved to busing tables as I demonstrated that I could manage the front of the house without causing problems. The work was unglamorous and the hours were long, but the environment was familiar in a way that school was not — the language, the food, the pace of a working kitchen. I was competent there in a way I was not yet competent in a classroom conducted entirely in English, and that competence mattered. It reminded me that the difficulty of one environment did not mean I was incapable.

After four semesters, my mother moved us to Minnesota because she could earn higher pay.

Minnesota was another world entirely. Los Angeles, for all its unfamiliarity, was warm and wide and full of people who had arrived from somewhere else. Minnesota was flat, quiet, and cold in a way that Los Angeles had not prepared me for — not the cold itself, which I had not yet experienced, but the cold as a permanent condition of the landscape, something the people around me had been negotiating their entire lives and had long since stopped noticing. We arrived in summer and it was pleasant enough, but even then, the sky looked different — a particular shade of pale blue that somehow communicated winter even in July.

My sister and I were the only Asian kids on the school bus. She was now at the same school.

The bus rides were quiet for us in a way that had nothing to do with noise. The other students talked and laughed and conducted the ordinary social business of adolescence. My sister and I sat together near the middle and watched. Some students looked at us with open curiosity, the uncomplicated kind that children have before they learn to disguise it. Others ignored us entirely. A few made attempts at conversation — single words offered s-l-o-w-l-y and loudly, as though speed and volume can make the words easier to understand. We answered with what we had, which was often not enough to sustain much, and the attempts usually trailed off into polite silence.

My sister handled it differently than I did. She was younger and more openly uncomfortable with the visibility of being different. I had already spent a year navigating an American high school, which had developed in me a certain tolerance for being observed. I did not enjoy the attention, but I had learned to treat it as information rather than judgment — a signal about the environment I was in, not a verdict on whether I belonged there.

I still understood only about half of what teachers said in class.

Without an interpreter, I developed other methods. I arrived early when I could and stayed after class when I did not understand an assignment. I copied notes carefully and compared them with what I found in the textbook, using the visual correspondence between the two to reconstruct the lesson's structure. When a student nearby seemed to understand something I did not, I found quiet ways to verify my own interpretation against theirs — not asking directly, which invited more interaction than I had language to sustain, but listening to how they worked through problems and adjusting my own approach accordingly. These were not sophisticated strategies. They were simply the strategies available to someone who needed to function before they were fully equipped to function.

But I learned other things.

I learned bowling and cross-country skiing in physical education. I watched classmates practice hockey on frozen lakes. There was a pleasure in those activities that had nothing to do with language — the body understood what to do in ways the mind was still catching up to, and competence in physical things created small openings in the social environment that competence in English could not yet provide.

I learned that waiting for public transit buses in frigid weather is not enjoyable. I learned that stepping into three-foot snow piles makes you walk quickly before moisture seeps into your shoes. I learned to dress in layers, which is knowledge that sounds trivial and is not.

I even learned to appreciate heavy metal music — specifically Def Leppard and AC/DC, which the students around me played constantly and which sounded like nothing I had ever heard in Taiwan. At first it was simply loud and incomprehensible. Gradually it began to make a kind of sense — not the sense of the lyrics, which

I could not yet follow, but the sense of the energy, the volume as communication, the particular satisfaction of music that did not require patience or quiet. It was another adaptation. It helped me fit in, and fitting in, even slightly, mattered.

During that year I worked weekends at the restaurant, busing tables and helping in the bar and kitchen.

Working in the bar was cleaner and earned tips, so I bought a copy of Mr. Boston Bartender's Guide and learned to mix cocktails. I did not ask Jimbo to train me. I bought the book, studied the drinks, practiced what I could, and was ready when the opportunity arrived to fill in. That pattern — prepare before you are asked, learn before the role is offered — had been forming since the receipt book days in my father's store. It was not strategy, exactly. It was simply the approach that felt natural given how I had been raised.

Whenever Jimbo, the bartender, was unavailable, I filled in.

Jimbo was in his late thirties, compact and unhurried, with the particular ease of a man who had found a job he understood well and had no ambition to complicate it. He was good at his work in the uncomplicated way that people are good at things they have been doing for a long time without thinking much about. He noticed things — when a customer needed another drink, when the ice was running low, when the room's temperature was shifting in a direction that required attention — with a kind of quiet peripheral awareness that I recognized because it resembled what I was practicing at the time in classrooms and on the school bus.

He liked me, I think, because I was useful and did not cause problems. He also seemed to appreciate, in the way that some adults do, that a sixteen-year-old working weekend bar shifts in Suburban Minnesota was probably managing more than was immediately visible.

The driving lesson happened in the parking lot behind the restaurant on a Sunday afternoon when the lot was empty. Jimbo had a manual-transmission Ford Fiesta that he drove as though it were an extension of himself, shifting without apparent thought, the clutch and gas working together in a way that seemed effortless until I was behind the wheel and discovered how many separate actions were being coordinated simultaneously.

When Jimbo was teaching me to drive, he had a cup of coffee in his right hand, likely due to the weather. He would drive with his left hand and even shift gears with his left hand. I never knew if he was trying to show me how easy it was to drive a manual transmission.

I stalled it immediately, and then twice more. Jimbo did not react the way I had seen adults react to mistakes — with impatience, or with the particular tiredness of someone who has explained the same thing too many times. He simply said, again, which meant we were doing it again, and I did it again, and eventually the car moved forward without dying, and he said, there, in the tone of a man confirming something that had never been in doubt.

We drove through the snow-covered mall parking lot for perhaps forty minutes, the car occasionally sliding and recovering in the way that manual cars in winter do. By the end I could keep it in motion through a stop sign and manage a turn without stalling. That was enough for one afternoon.

I did not have words at the time for what Jimbo was doing, and he would not have used words for it either. He was simply a man who had a skill and found it reasonable to pass it along to a kid who needed it. Looking back, that straightforward generosity — given without expectation of return, without ceremony, on an ordinary Sunday afternoon — was its own kind of lesson. Not about driving. About what it looks like when someone treats your development as a reasonable thing to invest an hour in.

As soon as the school year ended, we returned to sunny Southern California for my senior year in high school.

Before graduation, I sought programming courses and trade skills. I enrolled in one programming class at nearby community college before graduating high school. After the first class, classmates gathered at a pub across the street without me due to my age.

Computer work came naturally — I had wanted an Apple II since I was ten, had taught myself what the machine could do long before formal instruction was available, and the programming courses confirmed what I already suspected: that working with systems, understanding their logic, finding where they were efficient and where they were not, was something I was built for.

A vocational drafting course in high school surprised me more. There was something satisfying about the precision of it — the requirement to translate a three-dimensional object into an exact two-dimensional representation, with no room for approximation. The standards were absolute. Either the drawing was correct or it was not. I found that clarity restful in a way I had not anticipated.

Somewhere in those final months before graduation, something shifted. It was not dramatic. There was no single moment when confidence arrived. It was more that I looked back at what the previous two years had required — two cities, two climates, two school systems, multiple jobs, a language acquired through necessity rather than instruction — and realized that I had managed it. Not perfectly, and not easily. But I had managed it. And the skills I had accumulated in the process — the attention, the adaptability, the willingness to prepare before being asked — were not going away.

For the first time, I began to believe I could survive on my own — with my mind as well as my hands.

LESSON

Adaptation precedes confidence.

Opportunity presents to the willing and ready.

CHAPTER 4

Responsibility and Decision

> *Responsibility reveals whether competence can survive pressure and uncertainty.*

I received a rejection letter from every university I applied to — UCLA, UCSB, and Cal Poly. Cal State Los Angeles requested additional information before a decision could be made.

Meanwhile, friends in my circle were receiving acceptance letters from MIT, Stanford, and Yale.

Through conversations with those friends, I learned what I had not known: that college entrance essays were often written strategically, shaped to appeal to admissions offices in particular ways. I had simply told my life story in the most direct English I had, which at that point was roughly fifth-grade level. I had not understood that the essay was a performance as much as a document. That gap between what I had done and what the process required was not a failure of character. It was a failure of information.

I decided to attend community college for two years before transferring to a four-year university. That decision was easier to make than it might sound. I had been making practical adjustments my entire life — adapting to new schools, new cities, new languages, new jobs. One more adjustment in service of a longer goal was simply the next step in a pattern that had been forming since I was ten years old collecting newspaper payments at dinner hour. The path had changed. The direction had not.

By the time I entered community college, survival had already taught me how to work. What I had not yet learned was how trust is earned in professional environments — and how quickly it can be lost.

To support myself, I reduced my course load and took a job at a local travel agency as a porter. I started at the bottom — handling luggage, running errands, processing paperwork, doing whatever the office needed done before anyone with a more defined role arrived in the morning.

I did not view the work as beneath me. I viewed it as proximity. Every hour I spent in that building was an hour I could observe how the business actually operated — not how it was supposed to operate on paper, but how it did in practice, on ordinary days and under pressure. If I paid attention, I could learn. That had always been true. It was true here.

The travel business is governed by deadlines, documentation, and consequences. Visas must be correct. Flights must align. One mistake cascades quickly into the next, and the person who booked the wrong date is rarely present when the traveler discovers it at the check-in counter. I understood early that in this business, reliability was not a virtue among many. It was the primary one.

I learned the embassy and consulate process—what required appointments, what could be corrected, and what required starting over. Within a few months I could navigate that process faster than anyone else in the office. I arrived before the doors opened, filed paperwork in the order most likely to be processed the same day, and built working relationships with the clerks who determined the pace of approvals. Reliability built trust, and trust opened access that efficiency alone could not.

When winter arrived and tour volume slowed, I worried about losing my position. I asked to help wherever I could and was directed toward basic bookkeeping. I learned it the same way I had learned everything else — by doing it until it was no longer difficult, and then by paying attention to what came next.

Once bookkeeping became routine, I began listening closely to the travel consultants — how they structured complex routes, how they managed customer expectations when something went wrong, how they responded under the particular pressure of a problem that had a hard deadline and no clean solution. I learned by observing before participating. At the time that discipline felt unnatural, like restraint applied to something that wanted to move. Later I understood it differently: I was not waiting. I was accumulating.

I learned the airline and airport codes — the global reservation systems that governed every flight on every route in the industry. What had first appeared to be an arbitrary collection of letters gradually revealed its underlying logic, and once the logic was visible the entire system became navigable. I built fluency the way I had built it in language: through repetition, through necessity, through the particular motivation of someone who could not afford to remain a beginner.

Within a few months I was handling simple reservations independently. I even had a frequent corporate traveler to Japan asking for me specifically to process his itineraries. By the following season I was managing full outbound tour operations — building itineraries, coordinating accommodations, dispatching groups, solving the problems that arose between the schedule on paper and the reality of moving people through a country they did not know.

By twenty years old, I was the youngest tour operator in the area, trusted to secure hard-to-obtain accommodations inside Yellowstone National Park — a process that required months of advance planning, specific relationships with park concessionaires, and the kind of persistent follow-up that most operators found more effort than it was worth. I dispatched multiple busloads of tours each week. The operation ran, and it ran because I treated every detail as though someone was counting on it. Because they were.

That winter I learned a second airline reservation system and became proficient on both. I noticed that other operators were losing time to basic navigation — looking up commands, retracing steps, working around limitations they had not yet mapped. I compiled a practical reference guide: common commands, efficient sequences, workarounds for the errors that appeared most often. It was not a sophisticated document. It was useful, which was more important. People used it, and the operation ran faster because of it.

A larger, well-capitalized, more tour-focused agency took notice. A porter who I previously trained approached me as the existing agency was going through financial difficulties. I interviewed and was offered a position at one of their satellite offices to sell domestic tours. The conversation was direct, which I appreciated. They had observed what I could do and wanted it applied at a larger scale. I accepted.

Within a few months at the satellite office, I demonstrated my abilities and relocated to the headquarters to manage outbound tours.

The work was familiar in structure and larger in consequence — more groups, more complexity, more people whose travel depended on decisions I was making from a desk in a back office they would never see.

Soon after, I was asked to help integrate the outbound into inbound operations so that a single team could manage both. The logic was sound: separate teams meant duplicated infrastructure, communication gaps, and handoff errors that remained invisible until they became a passenger's problem. Integration would reduce those risks — provided the integration itself was designed carefully.

With integration came responsibility — without excuses.

Only after that responsibility was fully mine did I design a scheduling system to maximize bus utilization and reduce costs. The goal was efficiency: fewer dead miles, tighter turnaround times, each vehicle carrying close to full capacity on every run. On paper, the system worked. The numbers were clean. The logic was sound.

Until one day it wasn't.

It began with a major traffic delay on a route I had scheduled with no margin. One bus ran twenty minutes late into a transfer point. That twenty minutes pushed a second pickup past its window, which meant those passengers waited longer than expected, which prompted calls to the office, which divided my attention at the moment a third route required a driver decision that needed coordination. The radio channels meant to be sequential became simultaneous. Three conversations at once, each one urgent, none of them compatible with the attention the others required.

Mobile radio chatter from multiple buses at once.

Passengers were waiting.

Drivers were frustrated in traffic congestion.

And every decision now ran through me.

I made a decision on the first situation that freed one bus but delayed a group of passengers. I made a call on the second that resolved the passenger wait but created a scheduling conflict an hour later. Each decision I made in the first thirty minutes produced a consequence I was managing in the next thirty. I was not solving the problem. I was redistributing it.

Within two hours, the entire operation had unraveled. Multiple buses were affected, tens of travelers delayed or misdirected, the day's schedule no longer recoverable. Drivers were on the radio asking for instructions I did not have ready answers for. Passengers who had paid for an experience were managing an inconvenience instead, and the inconvenience was mine to own.

I owned it. There was nothing else to do.

What stayed with me afterward was not embarrassment. It was clarity.

I had confused efficiency with resilience. The system performed well when conditions cooperated. It had no tolerance for conditions that did not. I had optimized for the smooth version of the operation — the one where buses ran on time, traffic was predictable, and decisions could be made sequentially. I had not designed for the real version, where delays compound, attention is divided, and the system must absorb disruption without requiring a perfect response from the person managing it. That distinction had been invisible to me until the day it became unavoidable. I had been competent enough to build the system. I had not yet developed the judgment to stress-test it before trusting it with consequences that affected other people.

Competence earns opportunity, but judgment sustains responsibility.

From that point forward, I stopped asking whether a system worked when everything went right and began asking whether it could survive when things went wrong. Those are different questions, and the second is harder to answer honestly because it requires imagining failure before failure has occurred.

I redesigned the operation with buffers built into every segment — time margins that felt conservative on an ordinary day and proved necessary on a difficult one. I added redundancies: backup communication protocols, secondary contacts for each driver, escalation paths that did not route through a single person managing multiple channels simultaneously. I mapped the contingencies explicitly: if this route is delayed by more than fifteen minutes, this is the adjustment. If two routes are affected simultaneously, this is the priority sequence. The decisions that had been made reactively in the chaos of that afternoon became decisions made in advance, under no pressure, with full information available.

The redesigned system was not elegant. It had more moving parts than the original, more documentation, more apparent complexity. But it was honest — built for the operation as it existed, not for the operation as I wished it would behave. It ran without significant incident for the remainder of that season and the seasons that followed.

LESSON

Trust is accumulated slowly and lost quickly.

Stewardship requires systems that survive stress, not perfection.

CHAPTER 5

Influence and Credibility

> *Communication transfers belief before it transfers results.*

Texas was not a destination I had planned toward. It was the next place where the next opportunity presented itself, and by that point in my life I had learned that opportunities rarely arranged themselves according to plan. I had spent my formative years moving — Taiwan to Los Angeles, Los Angeles to Minnesota, Minnesota back to Southern California. One more relocation, this time voluntary and with more preparation than the others, felt less like disruption than like continuation.

What was different about Texas was that I arrived without the network I had spent years building in California. No professional relationships, no established reputation, no accumulated goodwill to draw on. Whatever I became here would be built from the beginning, which meant the beginning mattered more than usual.

I found work as a new car sales consultant at a Honda dealership. It was my first role where communication — not just execution — directly determined outcomes. Every other job I had held rewarded competence that was largely independent of whether the person in front of me chose to trust me. Sales was different. The outcome of every interaction depended on whether the customer believed what I was telling them, and whether they believed I understood what they needed.

The dealership floor had its own culture, which I studied the same way I had studied every other environment I entered — by watching before participating. The morning meetings established the day's targets and the previous day's rankings. The salespeople who had been there longest occupied a particular position on the floor, a physical territory as much as a professional one, and the newer consultants learned quickly which customers were fair game and which were understood to belong to someone else. I was not interested in that hierarchy for its own sake. I was interested in understanding how the environment worked so I could operate within it honestly.

I treated the position seriously. Sales was not a temporary job to me. It was a profession to understand — one with its own discipline, its own body of knowledge, its own standard of excellence that separated people who happened to sell cars from people who had genuinely learned how to help customers decide they would not regret.

I began by learning the product at a level most sales consultants did not bother with. I read the engineering specifications for every model on the lot — not because customers asked technical questions, but because deep product knowledge changed the quality of the conversation. When you understand why a feature exists and what problem it solves, you can explain it in terms of the customer's life rather than the brochure's language. That shift — from reciting specifications to explaining relevance — is the difference between a presentation and a conversation.

I drove every model available. I took customers on routes that demonstrated the specific qualities they had told me mattered to them.

If someone said they drove long distances for work, I showed them highway comfort. If someone said they had children, I showed them the features that would matter in three years, not just the features visible in the showroom today. Preparation before performance had served me in every environment I had entered. It served me here.

The dealership conference room doubled as a small library of training materials — binders, manuals, and a set of audio cassettes from a speaker I had never heard of before. The name on the cassette cases was Zig Ziglar. I borrowed the entire set.

I was not expecting much. I had encountered sales training material before, and most of it addressed tactics: how to handle objections, how to close, how to move a hesitant customer from consideration toward commitment. Useful in the way that any technical instruction is useful, but not particularly interesting. What came through the cassette player on my first morning commute was something different. The voice was warm and unhurried, and the first thing it addressed was not technique. It was character.

Ziglar taught that selling is not manipulation. It is the transfer of belief. If you genuinely believe in the value of what you offer, your responsibility is to communicate it clearly and honestly. If you do not believe in it, no amount of persuasion makes it right — and the customer, in time, will know the difference.

I rewound that section and listened to it again.

The distinction he was drawing was one I had felt but not yet articulated: the difference between influencing someone toward a decision that serves them and influencing someone toward a decision that serves you. The first is a form of service. The second is a form of extraction. They can look identical from the outside, especially in the short term. They produce entirely different outcomes over time — for the customer, for the relationship, and for the person doing the selling.

What stood out was not technique. It was ethics.

That framework reshaped how I viewed influence — not only in sales, but in every professional relationship that followed. I began applying it immediately: understanding what each customer needed, being honest when a different model served them better than the one they had come in to see, and declining to use pressure in moments when I knew the customer needed more time. That last part cost me some short-term transactions. I was certain then, and remain certain now, that it was the right approach.

As I learned the product and the process thoroughly, management asked me to help train new hires. I accepted without hesitation — not because I had spare time, but because I had learned in the travel agency that explaining something to someone else was the fastest way to discover whether you understood it.

Teaching forced clarity. If I could not explain something simply, I did not understand it well enough.

The training conversations I had with new hires followed a consistent pattern. I would explain a concept, watch them attempt to apply it, and then ask them what they thought had happened. That last step — asking them to interpret their own performance — was more useful than my interpretation of it. They knew what they had been trying to do. The gap between intention and execution was often more visible to them than to me. My job was to help them see it clearly and adjust, not to tell them what they had done wrong.

By setting reasonable expectations — being honest about how long it took to develop fluency with the product, how many conversations were needed before the process became natural — I reduced the frustration that caused most new consultants to disengage in their first weeks. Every trainee I worked with stayed longer than those trained by others, and several remained in the industry long after I had moved on. I do not take full credit for that. But I believe the consistency of the approach mattered.

I learned that credibility grows when competence is paired with consistency. It is not established by a single good interaction or a single impressive month. It is built by behaving the same way in the tenth conversation as in the first — with the same preparation, the same honesty, the same willingness to prioritize the customer's interest when it would be easier not to.

I also learned the quiet power of follow-up, through a project I initiated and which the dealership had not previously attempted.

The standard practice in car sales was to follow up with customers by phone after a purchase — a brief call to confirm satisfaction, which most customers experienced as a check-the-box exercise. I wanted to maintain contact in a way that was useful rather than procedural. The dealership agreed to cover postage if I could produce a customer newsletter, and I had the computer skills to make that possible.

I designed a simple monthly publication — two sides of a single sheet, clean layout, no graphics that required expensive printing. The content was practical: seasonal maintenance reminders, fuel efficiency tips, a brief note about common service items to watch as mileage accumulated. Nothing that required expertise to read, and nothing that read like an advertisement. I included my name and contact information at the bottom of every issue.

The newsletter went to every customer I had worked with, mailed on the same week each month. Most sales consultants considered the transaction finished when the customer drove off the lot. I treated it as the beginning of an ongoing relationship — one that I would maintain through consistent, useful contact until they were ready to make their next decision.

The results were not immediate, but they were durable. Customers began calling me directly when service questions arose, which meant I was present in their experience of owning the car, not just of buying it. Referrals followed — people who had received the newsletter passing my name to a family member or colleague who was considering a purchase. The newsletter created a compounding effect that a single good transaction could not: each month I stayed in contact, the relationship became slightly more established, and the next transaction became slightly more likely.

I did not fully understand at the time why it worked as well as it did. Looking back, the mechanism was simple: I was the only person in the customer's world who was consistently providing value related to a purchase they had already made. That consistency, maintained when there was nothing immediately to be gained from it, was read as reliability. Reliability, over time, becomes trust. Within four months, I came within a single transaction of earning Top Salesman of the Month — a distinction that went, that particular month, to a consultant who had been on the floor for three years and whose network had been compounding longer than mine.

I was not disappointed by the outcome. By then I had already learned the more important lesson: influence compounds when words align with actions over time. The month's ranking reflected four months of work. What I was building — the customer relationships, the referral network, the reputation for follow-through — would compound across years. The short-term measurement and the long-term investment were operating on different timescales, and I had made my choice about which one to optimize for.

I eventually moved on from the dealership, drawn toward opportunities in technology and eventually toward real estate — environments where the systems I was beginning to understand could be applied at larger scale. But the principle I had absorbed in that conference room and on those daily commutes did not leave with the job.

Influence is not about closing. It is about trust transferred gradually through reliability, clarity, and integrity.

LESSON

Everything communicates. Influence without integrity is manipulation. Trust grows when belief, words, and actions remain aligned — especially when outcomes are uncertain.

CHAPTER 6

Alignment Before Outcome

> *Alignment must precede outcome if success is to be sustained.*

For most of my life, I believed discipline and effort were enough. They carried me far — but not far enough.

By the time I had been operating businesses and managing investments for more than three decades, that belief had produced real results. Business and properties acquired, operations built, investors served, teams developed. The pattern of preparation before performance — formed in my father's store, refined in the travel agency, tested in the dealership and beyond — had compounded into something that looked, from the outside, like sustained success.

From the inside, something was beginning to feel insufficient.

As opportunities expanded, decisions grew heavier. Consequences widened. The people affected by my decisions were no longer just me — they were investors who had trusted me with capital, residents whose homes were under my management, partners whose reputations were attached to outcomes I was influencing. Competence had opened those doors. But I began to realize that competence alone does not govern ambition. Without restraint, even skill drifts. Left unchecked, capability becomes confidence, and confidence eventually seeks speed.

Del Walmsley once observed that the most dangerous leaders are those who have stopped listening — not because they lack intelligence, but because success has convinced them they no longer need anyone else's perspective.

I had been fortunate. The drift had not yet produced serious damage.

But I could see, with increasing clarity, that the framework I had been operating under — work hard, prepare thoroughly, execute reliably — was necessary but not complete. It addressed how to pursue an opportunity. It did not adequately address which opportunities should be pursued, or who bore the cost when the ones that looked right turned out not to be.

That question — who bears the cost — was the one I did not yet have a principled answer to.

After years of studying the Bible, I accepted Jesus Christ as my Savior. It was not a dramatic moment. It was a clarifying one.

Faith reframed ownership.

Opportunity became entrusted, not seized.

The risk did not disappear.

It clarified responsibility.

The practical effect was not immediate and it was not total. I did not wake the next morning with a different temperament or a different set of circumstances. What changed was the lens through which I evaluated what I was being offered and what I was being asked to carry. I had spent years asking whether an opportunity was achievable. I began asking whether it was mine to take — whether the consequences, if things went differently than planned, could be borne with integrity by the people involved, not just absorbed by the numbers on a spreadsheet.

That shift was not comfortable. It made certain decisions harder. It slowed some things that had been moving quickly. It raised questions I had previously moved past without fully answering. But it also produced something I had not anticipated: a coherence between what I believed, how I decided, and how I acted that had not fully existed before. That coherence did not guarantee outcomes. It did make the outcomes, whatever they were, easier to live with.

I began to evaluate decisions differently. Instead of asking how quickly something could scale, I asked who would bear the cost if it failed. Instead of asking whether a deal worked on paper, I asked whether I could carry its consequences with integrity. Faith did not make decisions easier. It made them heavier.

More than once, opportunities presented themselves that were defensible by conventional standards. The numbers worked. The participants were capable. Moving forward would have been rational—and easily justified.

But those same opportunities often relied on leverage with little margin for error, or commitments that transferred risk to others downstream. If assumptions failed, the consequences would not be shared evenly. That asymmetry was not something I could accept.

During a renovation phase described more fully in the next chapter — two apartment communities, a $2.5 million improvement budget — I was presented with additional acquisition opportunities that would have been attractive under ordinary circumstances. The properties were available at reasonable prices. The market conditions supported the thesis. Several people in my network were moving forward on similar deals and expected, reasonably, that I would participate.

The renovations already underway were more demanding than initial projections had suggested — not catastrophically, but in the way that significant construction projects always reveal complexity that was not fully visible at the time of underwriting. Carrying three newly acquired properties through a renovation cycle while underwriting additional acquisitions would have required leverage I was not comfortable with and attention I did not have available. The math was possible. The judgment required to execute it responsibly was not yet confirmed.

We chose to stay disciplined and complete the work required for the properties we already held.

In those moments, faith did not predict outcomes.

It governed restraint.

I chose not to proceed.

Those decisions slowed momentum.

They delayed growth.

They confused peers who expected participation.

But stewardship is not measured by how often we act.

It is measured by when we refuse to.

The social cost of that restraint was real and worth naming. In networks built around deal flow and momentum, declining to participate is read as hesitation or, worse, as a signal that you have lost confidence in a thesis the group shares. I was asked, more than once, whether something was wrong — whether I had information others did not, or whether my reluctance reflected a judgment about the specific opportunity that I was not sharing openly.

My answer was honest: nothing was wrong with the opportunity. Something was wrong with my capacity to steward it responsibly at that moment. That distinction — between an opportunity being good and an opportunity being right for you at a specific time — is one that conventional analysis does not capture, because it requires an honest accounting of your own limits, which is a different kind of analysis than underwriting a deal.

There was no external rulebook that would have faulted moving forward. But conviction imposed limits. Restraint preserved optionality, relationships, and peace long before results could validate the choice. Not every opportunity deserves pursuit. The ones that arrive when your capacity to carry them is already fully committed deserve particular scrutiny.

Alignment was tested not by success, but by uncertainty.

> *Restraint is not hesitation. It is conviction applied under pressure.*

There were other tests of alignment that arrived not through temptation but through injury.

A deal was taken from us through false misrepresentation — a situation in which information we had developed and a relationship we had built was used by another party in a way that was, at minimum, ethically indefensible. The details are not important here and the parties involved are not named. What is relevant is what the experience required of me at the time it happened.

The impulse to react was immediate and strong. I had been wronged in a manner that was documentable, and the instinct to pursue correction — through confrontation, through legal pressure, through a public accounting of what had occurred — was not unreasonable. Several people in my circle encouraged that response. The injustice was clear enough that most observers would have supported it.

Faith did not remove the disappointment. It prevented the reaction.

What I examined instead was whether pursuing correction, in the manner available to me, would produce a result commensurate with the cost — not the financial cost, but the cost in time, attention, relationship capital, and the particular kind of energy that prolonged conflict consumes. The answer, on honest examination, was no. The available paths to correction would have cost more than the deal itself was worth, and would have required me to become someone I did not want to be in the process of becoming.

I let it go. Not because it was just — it was not — but because holding it was more expensive than releasing it, and because the discipline required to release it was its own form of stewardship. I would rather lose a deal than lose the clarity that allowed me to evaluate the next one honestly.

There were partnerships I chose not to deepen, for similar reasons. The capability was present. The financial logic existed. What was absent was the value alignment that makes partnership durable under pressure. I had learned — from the bus operations failure, from a decade of watching partnerships strain and sometimes break at moments of maximum stress — that shared ambition is not the same as shared values. Shared ambition produces good outcomes when conditions cooperate. Shared values produce good outcomes when they do not.

Several of those decisions required declining relationships with people I respected and liked. That was not easy. But the clarity that came from evaluating partnerships through a values lens rather than a capability lens made the decisions less ambiguous, even when they were uncomfortable.

There were short-term gains I intentionally declined — situations in which an action that was technically permissible would have produced an outcome I could not defend to the people affected by it. The gains were real. The justifications were available. The constraint was internal, not external. No one would have known. I would have known, and I had learned by then that the person you become in the small decisions that no one is watching is the person who shows up in the large decisions that everyone is.

Alignment also changed how I responded when results fell short. I no longer rushed to force correction or recover appearances. When a renovation ran over budget, when occupancy lagged projections, when a market cycle moved against a position I held — my first question was no longer how to fix the optics but whether the original decision had been made with clarity, honesty, and genuine care for the people affected by it.

If the judgment had been sound and conditions had changed, I accepted the outcome without panic and adjusted. Outcomes are not always within your control. The quality of the decision that produced them is. If the judgment had been flawed — if I had known something I had not fully accounted for, or committed to something I should have examined more carefully — I corrected it without excuse. Not with performance of accountability, but with the actual work of making it right.

That distinction — between accepting outcomes that resulted from sound judgment and correcting outcomes that resulted from poor judgment — is one that alignment makes possible. Without a clear standard for how decisions should be made, every bad outcome feels like a verdict that requires defense. With that standard, a bad outcome can be examined honestly, which is the only way it can be learned from.

Faith became less about certainty and more about obedience — to principles, to people, and to process. It slowed decisions, widened perspective, and reminded me that stewardship is not proven by success, but by consistency when success is not guaranteed.

Alignment does not promise comfort. It provides coherence. When belief, judgment, and behavior remain aligned, outcomes compound without urgency — and peace becomes possible even when results lag.

That peace is not passivity. It is steadiness — the result of knowing the decision was made the right way, regardless of outcome. It allows you to be present to what is happening rather than managing the distance between what happened and what you wish had happened.

LESSON

Alignment must precede outcome.

Stewardship requires conviction strong enough to restrain action when momentum encourages speed.

CHAPTER 7

Stewardship in Practice

> *Stewardship begins long before results are visible.*

The renovation had been running for fourteen months when the calls started coming in about additional properties.

We were in the middle of a $2.5 million renovation across two multifamily communities — work that had been carefully underwritten and was proceeding on a timeline that left little room for the unexpected. Both properties were occupied during construction, which meant residents were managing inconvenience while we managed complexity. Every week brought decisions that required judgment I had not fully needed before: work sequencing, materials delays, city inspection scheduling, resident communication, investor reporting. The operation demanded full attention, and it was receiving it.

The additional properties that arrived during this period were genuinely attractive. Not marginal deals dressed up with optimistic projections — real opportunities with sound fundamentals, available at reasonable prices in markets I understood. Under different circumstances, the argument for moving forward would have been straightforward.

The circumstances were exactly what they were: two properties mid-renovation, a team operating near capacity, and a capital position that could support expansion on paper but not absorb the consequences if expansion and renovation encountered stress simultaneously.

We chose restraint.

The opportunity was real—but stewardship demanded patience.

That decision was not celebrated. It was questioned. People who had expected us to move forward asked what had changed. Nothing had changed. That was precisely the point. The conditions had not changed. Our capacity had not grown.

The discipline required was the discipline of declining something good because we were already committed to something we had not yet finished doing well.

The decision cost us several attractive acquisitions in the short term.

Roughly six months later, we executed our pre-planned refinance. The proceeds allowed us to return 101% of investors' original capital.

In hindsight, that restraint protected the portfolio when the market tightened eighteen months later.

John C. Maxwell teaches the Law of the Big Mo: when momentum builds, leadership becomes easier and opportunities multiply. Progress begins to feed on itself. I have seen that law operate exactly as described. It is accurate.

What Maxwell's observation does not address — and what experience eventually supplied — is what momentum can do to judgment when it is not governed by discipline.

Momentum creates its own kind of pressure. Opportunities begin to appear faster than judgment can comfortably evaluate them. One of the clearest examples in my own experience came several years earlier.

After three car wash acquisitions, a call came through my real estate broker, Evelyn, from the bank that held the note on my existing car wash operations.

The bank had a problem. A borrower had stopped making payments across a small portfolio of self-service car wash locations spread throughout the Dallas-Fort Worth metroplex. The bank was moving toward foreclosure and needed someone with operational experience to step in at the loan balance — someone who knew the business, understood the equipment, and could manage the transition without the properties deteriorating further. They thought of me.

The framing mattered. This was not a cold opportunity from an unknown source. It came through a trusted channel, from an institution that knew my track record, asking whether I was willing to apply experience I already had to a situation that needed exactly that experience. The logic was clean. The timing felt right. The income expansion was real. I said yes.

I received the details and reviewed the numbers. Six locations. Revenue figures that supported the thesis. A portfolio that, on paper, made sense to operate.

As it turned out, the paper did not match the reality on properties.

The previous borrower had been an absentee owner — a man who had acquired the locations as an investment rather than an operation and had managed them from a distance, or not at all. What absentee ownership produces is predictable: neglected equipment, inconsistent maintenance, and revenue figures that look stable on paper but deteriorate quickly under inspection. I had to deliver the bad news to the bank and renegotiate the purchase price. The renegotiation ultimately produced a $1,000,000 reduction in the purchase price.

The equipment required upgrades at nearly every location — not catastrophic failures, but the kind of accumulated neglect that cannot be addressed quickly or cheaply. The revenue figures I had been given reflected what the locations had once produced, or what they might produce under attentive management, not what they were producing on the day I took responsibility for them. The difference was significant.

I made one decision immediately: the farthest location had to go. A single site that required two hours of round-trip travel to monitor or address was not an asset under these conditions — it was a liability that would consume time the other five locations needed. I arranged the sale and moved on.

What remained was five locations spread across a metroplex large enough that driving between them consumed substantial portions of every day I spent on them. And they required presence. Self-service car wash operations are, by their nature, vulnerable to theft — not dramatic theft, but the persistent, low-visibility kind that an absentee owner had not been deterring and that a new operator had to address immediately and repeatedly. Cash handling, equipment access, site monitoring — each location required systems and oversight that I was now responsible for maintaining across a geography that resisted consolidation.

I was stretched thin in a way I had not been before. Not beyond function — the operations continued, the locations ran, the situation did not collapse. But the time and attention the portfolio demanded was time and attention that was not available for anything else. I was managing a correction across five locations while trying to identify what the portfolio could eventually become, and the gap between those two tasks did not close quickly.

We operated for several more years. Each location was eventually sold individually — not as a portfolio exit, but one at a time, as redevelopment interest arrived for each specific site. The exits were not losses — the land held value that the operations, in their condition, had not fully reflected. But the years between acquisition and exit were years of management intensity I had not fully underwritten when I said yes to the bank's call through Evelyn. The income expanded slowly but never to the level shown on the paperwork. It cost more to maintain, and demanded more of my capacity than the opportunity had appeared to require.

What I had mistaken for a well-framed opportunity was, in part, a well-framed problem — one that the bank needed solved and that I had the right background to solve, but that I had not examined with the same rigor I would later apply to every significant commitment. The trusted channel, the flattering framing, and the familiar business category had done what they do: they had made yes feel prudent rather than prompting the harder questions. What does this portfolio actually look like on the ground? What did absentee ownership cost it that the numbers do not show? What will it require of my time and attention at precisely the scale and geographic spread being offered?

I had not yet developed the habit of asking those questions before the decision rather than after it. I had the experience to recognize the answers once I was inside the operation. What I had not yet built was the discipline to require the answers before I committed.

That distinction — between experience and discipline, between knowing what to look for and building the practice of looking before you move — is what the car wash expansion taught.

I had no clean label for what the car wash expansion had been when it was happening. I knew it had moved faster than my judgment warranted. I knew the individual decisions had each seemed reasonable while the aggregate had not. But I did not have a name for the pattern until sometime later, when Christian Hilliard gave me one in a setting I had not expected.

Christian is a friend, investor, and advisor whose observations I respect over the years. He does not moralize. He describes what he sees, directly and without decoration, and trusts the listener to draw what they need from it. The name he gave me came not from theory but from his own household.

Christian had partnered with his son to start a new business — acquiring small, owner-operated businesses — the kind too small for institutional attention, available when a founder is ready to exit but has no obvious buyer. The son had identified the market, developed a process for reaching owners, and built a pipeline of conversations running simultaneously. Closings began to follow — one, then another, then another. The momentum was real and the results were visible. Each acquisition made sense on its own terms. The son was doing what capable people do when something is working: he kept doing it.

What was not being monitored, as the pipeline grew and the closings accelerated, was the capital the aggregate required. Each individual deal had its own funding logic. Each one passed its own test. But the sum of the commitments was growing in ways that the individual view of each deal did not reveal — and capital requirements, unlike deal flow, do not wait for a convenient moment to surface.

When Christian described this in the group, he was not telling a story with a resolved ending. The situation was still in motion. He was not packaging a lesson — he was describing something he was watching unfold in real time, in a business he had helped his son build. That is part of why it landed the way it did. A cautionary tale with a clean ending can be heard and set aside. A situation still unresolved asks something different of the listener.

He called it "deal junkie."

The term is precise in a way that more clinical language is not. A junkie is not someone who made a single bad decision. A junkie is someone whose relationship with the thing has changed — someone for whom the pursuit has become its own justification, independent of whether the underlying logic still holds. The son was not reckless. He was not unintelligent. He was someone for whom the process of acquiring had become easy enough that ease had substituted for evaluation. The pipeline felt like progress. The closings felt like confirmation. The capital question arrived late because no individual deal had raised it.

I recognized it in the group setting without saying so. Not because I had done exactly what the son was doing, but because I understood the mechanism from the inside. The car wash expansion had not been a pipeline of acquisitions — it was a single decision, one lender, one call through Evelyn. But the structure of the error was the same. Each location had seemed manageable individually. The geographic spread, the equipment condition, the overstated revenue, the theft exposure across five sites — none of those had announced themselves as a collective problem at the moment of commitment. They had each been a separate consideration, each one addressable in isolation, each one insufficient on its own to reverse a decision that had already been framed as an opportunity rather than a commitment.

The aggregate is always the actual commitment. The individual view of each component is what momentum offers you in place of that accounting — a series of manageable pieces that adds up to something you did not fully underwrite. What makes the deal junkie pattern genuinely dangerous is not that the individual decisions are wrong. It is that they are right enough, each on their own terms, to keep passing the test that should be applied to the whole.

That is what momentum substitutes for judgment: it replaces the question of what the aggregate requires with the much easier question of whether the next step is defensible. And the next step almost always is. That is why the pattern is so difficult to interrupt from the inside. Each decision feels like discipline. The accumulation is the problem, and the accumulation only becomes visible when you stop moving long enough to count what you are actually carrying.

Christian did not tell the group what his son would do next, or how the situation would resolve. He named the pattern, described it honestly, and left it there. That was enough. The name stuck — not because it was clever, but because it described something real that most people in that room had either experienced or were at risk of experiencing, and that most people in investment communities do not have clean language for. Momentum is celebrated. The cost of unexamined momentum is not.

Stewardship is not experience applied. It is a structure of questions maintained even when the opportunity feels familiar, even when the source is trusted, even when the logic is sound.

The renovation restraint that opened this chapter was not instinctive. It was the product of having learned, the hard way, what moving before that structure is in place actually costs.

Stewardship sometimes requires the opposite instinct.

Momentum can tempt leaders to expand simply because conditions appear favorable. Discipline asks a harder question — not whether we can continue, but whether we should.

> *Momentum invites expansion. Stewardship determines whether expansion is wise.*

Stewardship is not a philosophy. It is a discipline practiced before outcomes are visible.

The stories in this chapter — the renovation, the car wash locations, Christian's account of his son — are not cautionary tales. They are descriptions of what stewardship looks like when it is absent, and what it costs when its absence goes unrecognized long enough to compound.

What they point toward is not a set of practices, though practices follow. They point toward something that precedes practice — an orientation that is either present before a decision begins or is not present at all. You cannot apply it after the fact. You cannot retrieve it once momentum has already replaced it. It has to be the condition from which decisions are made, not the correction applied when decisions go wrong.

That orientation is made of three things that cannot be separated from each other without losing all three.

The first is humility — not the performed kind that names itself in conversations, but the functional kind that changes how a decision is approached before anyone is watching. Functional humility begins with a recognition: the capital, the trust, the relationships, the residents, the investors — none of it is yours in the sense that you created it independently of everyone who contributed to it. You are a steward of it. That recognition is not diminishing. It is clarifying. It narrows the question from what can I do with this to what does this require of me — and those are not the same question, and they do not produce the same decisions.

The second is accountability — the prior knowledge, held honestly before a commitment is made, that others will carry the consequences of what you decide. Not abstractly. Specifically. The investor whose retirement timeline is attached to your underwriting. The resident whose home is under your management. The team member whose livelihood depends on the operation you are building.

Accountability of this kind is not a burden applied from outside. It is a standard accepted from within, and it functions as a governor on the kind of analysis that momentum encourages — the analysis that starts with the conclusion and works backward to justify it.

The third is discipline — the habit, maintained consistently and not only under pressure, of asking the harder question before the easier one. The easier question is whether the opportunity is attractive. The harder question is whether you are prepared to steward it responsibly at this moment, with the capacity you actually have, for the people who will actually be affected. The car wash expansion passed the easier question. It had not been subjected to the harder one. The renovation restraint required holding the harder question in place against the pull of conditions that made the easier answer feel sufficient.

These three — humility, accountability, discipline — are not a sequence. They do not operate independently or in rotation. Humility without accountability produces good intentions that do not adequately count the cost to others. Accountability without discipline produces awareness of responsibility that does not survive the pressure of an attractive opportunity. Discipline without humility produces process that serves the operator rather than the people the operator is responsible to. Together, as a single orientation maintained before decisions begin, they produce something that none of them produces alone: the capacity to evaluate what you are actually being asked to carry, rather than what the opportunity appears to offer.

The practices described in the chapters that follow are not techniques to be applied situationally. They are expressions of this orientation made operational — what humility, accountability, and discipline look like when they are built into the structure of how decisions are made rather than residing only in the intentions of the person making them. The orientation without the practices remains personal. The practices without the orientation become mechanical. Neither is sufficient. Together, they are what stewardship in practice actually requires.

LESSON

Stewardship is not a response to pressure. It is an orientation formed before pressure arrives — in humility, accountability, and discipline maintained before any decision begins.

CHAPTER 8

The Seven Practices of Stewardship

> *Principles guide leadership, but practices sustain it.*

There is a distance between knowing what stewardship requires and building an operation that practices it — reliably, without exception, in the presence of people other than yourself.

I crossed that distance slowly, and not without mistakes. The principles described in the preceding chapters were formed through experience. But experience produces principles, not systems. A principle tells you what matters. It does not tell the person next to you what to do when you are not in the room.

That gap — between a leader's conviction and an organization's consistent behavior — is where most stewardship fails. Not from dishonesty. Not from lack of intention. But from the assumption that what is clear to you is therefore clear to those around you, and that values held privately will express themselves publicly without being deliberately built into the structure of how decisions are made.

Over time I learned that they will not.

The seven practices that follow are the operational form of the principles this book describes. Each one can be traced to a specific failure or a specific pressure that made visible what had not yet been made structural. None of them arrived as insight. They arrived as correction — the kind that comes from watching something go wrong and understanding, with uncomfortable clarity, exactly why.

They are not a formula. A formula assumes conditions will cooperate. These practices were designed for conditions that do not.

1. Downside Before Upside

Every decision begins with downside risk. I ask what can go wrong before imagining what might go right. If a project cannot survive reasonable stress — delays, cost overruns, or human error — it is not ready.

This practice was not instinctive. It was learned through an early acquisition in which the upside analysis was thorough and the downside analysis was not. The property's income projections were built on an occupancy assumption that was reasonable for the market in stable conditions. What the analysis did not adequately account for was what the property's income looked like at eighty percent occupancy during a renovation that required temporarily relocating some residents. The upside case was accurate. The path to the upside case ran through a period that the upside case had not fully described.

From that point forward, I began every underwriting exercise with a stress scenario rather than ending with one. What does this property look like at seventy percent occupancy? What does the debt service coverage ratio look like if renovation runs thirty percent over budget and takes six months longer than projected? What is the cash position at month eighteen if lease-up velocity is half of what the market suggests it should be? Those are not pessimistic questions. They are honest ones. A project that can answer them without producing a result that is unacceptable to the people invested in it is a project that is ready to proceed. A project that cannot answer them is a project that requires more work before capital is committed.

2. Protection Before Optimism

Renovations rarely unfold exactly as planned. Delays, labor shortages, material lead times, and hidden conditions quickly test every assumption. Optimism without protection is not confidence. It is exposure.

The $2.5 million renovation taught this more concretely than any underwriting exercise could. The original scope had been developed through careful inspection and contractor bidding. It was a reasonable scope based on reasonable information. What the inspection had not revealed — because it could not, without opening walls — was the extent of deferred maintenance in the electrical and plumbing systems of the older of the two properties. When the work reached that stage, the scope expanded. The budget expanded with it.

The expansion was manageable because protection had been built in advance. The renovation budget included a contingency reserve that most operators would have considered conservative. It was not conservative enough to absorb the full overrun without adjustment, but it was sufficient to absorb it without crisis — without calling investors for emergency capital, without making decisions under financial pressure that would have compromised the quality of the work. The contingency was not a sign of pessimism in the original underwriting. It was a sign of honesty about what renovations of that age and complexity reliably produce.

Optimism about outcomes is appropriate. Optimism about the path to outcomes is expensive. The distinction between the two is what protection is designed to maintain.

3. Liquidity Creates Judgment

Cash reserves are not idle capital. They are respect — for investors, employees, and residents. Liquidity buys time, and time allows judgment. I would rather explain why capital is waiting than explain why it is gone. Reserves create space for correction without panic and decisions without coercion.

The most direct way I can describe the value of liquidity is this: it determines whether a decision can be made at the right time or only at the available time. Those are not the same.

During one period of our portfolio's operation, a property required a capital expenditure that had not been planned in the current period's budget — a roof replacement that an inspection had assessed as manageable within two years, but which produced a significant leak during a weather event that moved the timeline. The decision to address it properly rather than temporarily required capital. Because operating reserves had been maintained at a level that felt conservative during months when nothing was wrong, the decision could be made on the merits: what does this property need, and what is the right way to address it? Not: what is the cheapest thing we can do this month that will allow us to address this later?

The residents in that building experienced the repair as a property that was well managed. The investors in that property received communication that described a necessary expenditure being handled appropriately. Neither outcome was possible without the liquidity that made the decision available at the right moment. That is what I mean when I say cash reserves are not idle capital. They are the capacity to make the right decision when the right decision is required.

4. Conservative Leverage

Leverage magnifies outcomes, both good and bad. Used carefully, it accelerates progress. Used aggressively, it transfers risk to those least able to absorb it. I prefer conservative leverage that preserves margin for error and strategic optionality. Growth that requires perfection to succeed is not growth — it is fragility. Asymmetry improves the probability of success while limiting downside risk.

The clearest illustration of this principle in my experience was not a deal I took but one I declined. The opportunity was structured at a loan-to-value ratio that was conventional for the asset class and the period — not unusual, not aggressive by market standards. The acquisition price was fair in comparison. The business plan was credible. The projected returns were attractive.

What the leverage structure required, on honest examination, was that three separate assumptions hold simultaneously: that interest rates remained stable, that the renovation was completed within the projected timeline, and that lease-up velocity matched the market's historical average for comparable properties. Each assumption was individually reasonable. The requirement that all three hold simultaneously was a different matter. Leverage transforms the conjunction of reasonable assumptions into a single fragile dependency. If any one assumption failed, the margin for correction was insufficient.

I declined the opportunity. The decision cost a return that, as it turned out, was achieved by those who moved forward — conditions cooperated, assumptions held, the deal performed. I do not consider that evidence that the decision was wrong. It is evidence that the conditions were favorable. Favorable conditions do not validate a structure that would have been dangerous if conditions had been otherwise. Stewardship is not measured by outcomes in favorable conditions. It is measured by what happens when conditions are not.

5. Systems Before Heroics

Systems matter more than intentions alone. I design operations to function without heroics. Clear processes, documented procedures, and redundancy protect people from fatigue and prevent small problems from becoming large ones. A system that depends on exceptional individuals is not strong — it is vulnerable.

I learned the cost of heroics early, in the travel agency operations described in Chapter 4, when a scheduling system designed for efficiency rather than resilience collapsed under the ordinary pressure of a single delay. That lesson was formative. It did not fully transfer without repetition.

Years later, managing a property portfolio during a period when a key team member became unexpectedly unavailable for several weeks, I discovered how much of our operational continuity had been residing in one person's knowledge and judgment rather than in documented systems. Processes that we believed were organizational turned out to be personal. Vendors were managed through relationships that person held. Resident issues were resolved through judgment that person had developed and not yet transferred. The operation continued, but it required more effort from everyone else than it should have, and several things that should have been routine required improvisation.

The redesign that followed was unglamorous. It involved documenting processes that experienced operators found tedious to describe because the knowledge had become automatic. It involved building redundancy into vendor relationships so that no single contact failure could interrupt service. It involved creating escalation paths that did not depend on any specific individual being available. None of this was interesting work. All of it was necessary, and the operation was measurably more resilient after it was done.

A system that depends on exceptional people performing consistently is not a system. It is a collection of dependencies. The goal is operations that function well when ordinary people apply them consistently — because that is what operations are made of, on most days, in most circumstances.

6. Communication Before Comfort

Communication precedes comfort. Bad news does not improve with age. Transparency builds trust long before it is needed. I would rather disappoint early with honesty than surprise late with consequences. Silence may delay discomfort, but it multiplies cost.

The instinct to delay difficult communication is nearly universal, and I have not been immune to it. The specific temptation in real estate operations is to wait until a problem has been resolved before disclosing that it existed — to deliver the news and the solution simultaneously, which feels more competent than delivering the news alone. That instinct is understandable and wrong.

One evening, smoke was billowing out of an apartment unit. A resident called 911. Another resident banged on the door of a team member who lived in that community. Shortly, the fire department nearby arrived with three fire engines. Firefighters forced their way through the door and extinguished the fire in the living room. By the time the community manager arrived, one fire fighter walked out of the unit with a burnt laptop in his hand.

I was notified when the manager was on her way to the community. My instinct was to wait until more information was available before communicating to investors. That would have taken another two to three days or up to a week.

I communicated immediately with the limited information I had. We had no resolution yet. We did not yet have the cause of the fire. The investor communication was direct: here is what we have encountered, here is what it means to occupancy, what we can do from here on out. We do not yet have a resolution, but we were already caring for the affected residents and would follow with more information as it became available.

The response was not what the event predicted — alarm, loss of confidence, difficult questions I was not ready to answer. The response was, almost uniformly, appreciation for the directness. Several investors said explicitly that the early communication increased their confidence rather than reducing it. What they heard was not that something had gone wrong. What they heard was that they were being treated as partners who deserved accurate information rather than as audiences who deserved a polished narrative.

That experience confirmed what I had understood in principle: trust is not built by the absence of problems. It is built by how problems are handled. Early, honest communication about a manageable difficulty produces more trust than late, polished communication about a difficulty that has been resolved. The former treats investors as partners. The latter treats them as a constituency to be managed.

7. Patience Before Expansion

Stewardship requires patience. Growth that arrives too quickly often demands compromises that surface later. I measure success less by speed and more by sustainability. Expansion that outpaces judgment eventually demands correction — and correction is always more expensive than restraint.

The period following the renovation's completion was a period of deliberate consolidation. The properties had been improved. Occupancy had stabilized. The team had been tested and had performed. The natural instinct — reinforced by the momentum that had built during the renovation — was to move immediately toward the next acquisition.

We did not. We spent the better part of a year ensuring that the systems built during the renovation were functioning without the intensity that renovation demands. We evaluated what had worked and what needed refinement. We rebuilt operating reserves that the renovation had drawn down. We assessed the team's capacity honestly, not optimistically. We answered the question that expansion pressure tends to suppress: are we actually ready, or do we simply feel ready because momentum suggests we should be?

That pause was not popular. It read, from the outside, like hesitation. It was not hesitation. It was the discipline of completing one thing before beginning another — of confirming that what had been built would endure before adding weight to it. The acquisitions that followed that period were underwritten with better judgment, executed with better systems, and managed by a team that had been adequately prepared rather than immediately redeployed.

Patience in this context is not passivity. It is the recognition that the capacity to steward what you have determines the wisdom of acquiring more. Speed of acquisition without depth of execution is not growth. It is the accumulation of problems at a pace that exceeds the capacity to address them.

None of these practices are theoretical. They were learned through mistakes, through pressure, and through the particular accountability that comes from managing capital and operations on behalf of people who trusted the judgment behind both. I repeat them not because they are easy, but because they work — not in every market cycle, not in every circumstance, but consistently enough across enough cycles that they have become the structure within which all other decisions are made.

I do not assume I will always be right. That humility shapes how decisions are structured from the beginning. I leave room for error, for learning, and for adjustment. The goal is not to eliminate risk — it is to ensure that when risk materializes, it is survivable, and that the people who trusted me with their capital can say, accurately, that I did not make their situation worse through negligence or recklessness.

That standard — survivable risk, honest process, protection before performance — is what each of these seven practices is designed to maintain. None of them prevent difficulty. All of them prevent difficulty from becoming catastrophe.

Stewardship is quiet.

It rarely announces itself.

It appears in preparation, in margins that seem conservative, and in decisions that protect people and capital even when no one is watching. Over time, those choices compound — not just financially, but relationally and reputationally. The investors who have stayed with us across multiple cycles did not stay because returns were always as projected. They stayed because when things were difficult, we handled the difficulty the same way we handled everything else: with honesty, with care for their interests, and with the patience to wait for the right decision rather than the convenient one.

There is a version of stewardship that is performed — communicated in investor presentations, described in mission statements, referenced in conversations where it earns approval. That version is not what I am describing. The stewardship that produces durable outcomes is not performed. It is practiced — in the decisions no one sees, in the restraint that earns no recognition, in the communication that delivers news no one wanted to hear. It shows up in preparation rather than in announcements, and its effects accumulate long before they are visible to anyone outside the work.

Durable outcomes are never accidental. They are the result of repeated, disciplined judgment applied long before outcomes are visible.

Stewardship is not proven by control, but by the ability to entrust responsibility to others — and to have built the systems, the trust, and the judgment required for that entrustment to be something more than hope.

LESSON

Stewardship is practiced before outcomes are known.

Durable outcomes come from disciplined judgment long before success becomes visible.

CHAPTER 9

Partnership and Multiplication

> *Partnership multiplies capacity only when character and value align.*

I did not build alone.

Every meaningful expansion in my life came through partnership. Not all partnerships were equal, and not all were successful. Over time, I learned that alignment matters more than capability. Skill can be taught. Character rarely is.

That lesson arrived early, and it arrived in a form I had not anticipated.

During my early years in Texas, before the real estate portfolio had taken shape, I was looking for businesses that could generate seasonal income with manageable overhead. The concept was straightforward: a fireworks stand positioned outside my gas station that sold beer and wine, on a high-traffic road, timed to the two peak retail windows — July 4th and Christmas. In Texas, fireworks retail is a licensed, time-limited operation. Each holiday window runs roughly ten days. There is no recovering a missed opening date. The inventory is perishable in the most literal sense — once the holiday passes, the demand disappears entirely.

I had the location, the license, and the inventory sourced. What I needed was help building the stand itself. I hired a seasoned carpenter who came with a solid portfolio of completed work. His skills were not in question.

He showed up on time and ready on the first day. The work was correct — the framing was sound, the measurements were accurate, the structure was taking shape on schedule.

Then the excuses began.

He started to miss days and arrived late. By the end of the first week the work was behind, and by the middle of the second week I understood why: he was arriving having already been drinking. Not visibly impaired in the way that produces obvious errors, but impaired in the way that produces unreliability — the diminished urgency, the shortened days, the receding commitment to a deadline that was not his deadline.

I ended the arrangement. The conversation was difficult — he was belligerent and insisted on being paid for the full amount of the incomplete work. The police were called and a criminal trespassing warning was issued. I settled what I owed him for the work completed and sent him on his way. What remained was a partially built stand, an approaching deadline, and the clear understanding that I was the only person available to finish it.

I finished it. The stand opened on time. The season produced what it was designed to produce.

What stayed with me was not the inconvenience of finishing alone. It was the clarity about what the hiring decision had missed. I had evaluated the carpenter on the dimension he presented well — craftsmanship, experience, references that spoke to the quality of his work. I had not evaluated him on the dimension that would determine whether he could meet a hard deadline under conditions he had not set. Those are different assessments of different things, and I had performed only one of them.

> *Skill may open the door, but character determines whether someone can stay in the room.*

That observation seems obvious in retrospect. It was not obvious before I had learned it. And it is the kind of lesson that does not transfer completely through hearing it stated — it requires being in the situation where the skill is present and the character is not and experiencing the specific consequence that produces.

Early on, I thought effort could compensate for misalignment. I believed that if someone had the right skills and worked hard enough, the values could be worked around or developed over time. Experience corrected that assumption, and it corrected it more than once.

When pressure arrives — and it always does — character surfaces. The differences in values, risk tolerance, and accountability that seemed manageable in ordinary conditions express themselves through decisions when conditions are not ordinary. A partner who manages risk differently than you do is not a problem when everything is going well. That difference becomes the central fact of the partnership the first time something goes wrong and the two of you must decide how to respond.

I learned to watch for this in early conversations. Not the conversations where someone described their strengths and their vision — those conversations are easy and almost everyone handles them well. The revealing conversations were the ones about difficulty: how someone had handled a deal that had gone against them, what they had done when a partner had not performed as expected, how they described a failure and who they understood to be responsible for it. Those conversations told me more about who someone was than any amount of resume review or reference checking.

What I was listening for was not perfection. I was not looking for people who had never made mistakes or faced adversity — those people do not exist, and if they claimed so, that claim itself was informative. I was listening for honesty about what had happened and what they had learned, for accountability that was genuine rather than performed, and for a relationship with uncertainty that was realistic rather than either dismissive or paralyzed.

As my responsibilities increased, so did my selectivity. This was not the result of diminished trust, but of deeper understanding. I had more to protect — not just my own interests, but the interests of investors, residents, and team members whose outcomes were affected by the partnerships I chose. That accountability made the evaluation more careful.

Partnership is stewardship of trust. It requires clarity, boundaries, and accountability from the beginning — not because good partnerships are adversarial, but because unaddressed assumptions have a way of becoming expensive exactly when a partnership is under pressure and can least afford the cost.

The most instructive partnership difficulty I have experienced was not one that ended in conflict. It was one that drifted — a situation in which two people who had started with compatible values and genuine respect for each other allowed the operating assumptions of their arrangement to remain unexamined for long enough that when a significant decision arrived requiring alignment, they discovered they had developed different understandings of what they had agreed to. Neither person had been dishonest. Both had been insufficiently explicit. The resolution required more time, more legal involvement, and more relational cost than it would have required if the original conversation had been more thorough.

From that point forward, I began any significant partnership with a more deliberate conversation — not a legal document, though documentation followed, but a direct exchange about how we would handle the situations that documentation does not anticipate: a disagreement about whether to hold or sell, a period of underperformance, a moment when one party wants to move faster and the other wants to wait. Those conversations are uncomfortable when everything is going well because they require imagining scenarios no one wants to inhabit. They are invaluable when those scenarios arrive, because they have already been thought through.

I learned to communicate expectations early and to address misalignment quickly. Delaying difficult conversations does not preserve harmony — it compounds cost. The conversation that would have taken thirty minutes in February costs three months and a great deal of goodwill in November.

Not every partnership deepened. Some remained transactional, which is its own legitimate form of professional relationship. Others ended, for reasons that varied but that shared a common pattern: the misalignment that had been manageable in favorable conditions became unmanageable when conditions changed.

One partnership ended after a period of market difficulty revealed that the other party's risk tolerance was significantly lower than what our operating strategy required. This was not a character failure — the person was honest, capable, and had operated in good faith throughout. The alignment gap was genuine, and in calmer markets it had been bridgeable through conversation. Under sustained pressure, the gap produced different responses to the same information: where I saw a period requiring patience, they saw a period requiring exit. Neither position was unreasonable. They were incompatible.

The ending of that partnership was handled with care and mutual respect, which I believe was possible because both parties had been honest throughout about the difficulty they were experiencing. There was no accumulation of grievance to navigate, no competing narrative to manage. There was simply a recognition that the arrangement had reached the limit of what it could serve well, and an agreement to conclude it cleanly.

Alignment is not proven by agreement. It is proven by how differences are handled when the stakes rise. A partnership that ends cleanly, with clarity and respect, is not a failure. A partnership that ends in litigation, or in silence, or in the slow deterioration of something that should have been addressed directly — that is a more expensive outcome, and it is usually avoidable.

Mentorship followed naturally from the accumulation of experience. Not as a role I sought, but as a responsibility that arrived with the credibility that experience eventually provides.

I have been a mentor in the Lifestyles Unlimited community for three years, working with investors who are at various stages of building their own portfolios — some acquiring their first property, some managing a handful, some working toward the kind of operation that can function independently of constant owner involvement, and others who invested passively without taking on operational responsibilities. What I observed early in that position was that the most common thing new investors needed was not information. Information was available. What they needed was a framework for making decisions when the information was incomplete, which is the condition under which most real consequential decisions are made.

I never viewed mentorship as creating followers. The goal was always independent judgment. A mentor who is needed indefinitely has not multiplied anything — they have created a dependency that constrains the person they intended to develop and makes the relationship's continuity more important than the person's growth.

The discipline I learned, and tried to practice, was to teach process rather than to prescribe outcomes. Outcomes are situational. What works in this market cycle, with this capital structure, for this specific property in this specific location, may not work in different conditions — and the investor who has learned to copy a successful outcome without understanding the process that produced it will be poorly equipped when the conditions change, which they always do.

One early mentee illustrated this clearly. He was analytical, thorough, and had done more preparation before his first acquisition than most investors do before their third. What he struggled with was the moment of decision — the transition from analysis to commitment, which requires accepting that the information will never be complete and that judgment must operate in the gap. He kept returning to me with additional analysis, each round more detailed than the last, each one delaying the decision without meaningfully reducing the uncertainty.

The conversation that mattered was not about the specific deal. It was about what analysis is for. Analysis reduces known risks and identifies unknown ones. It does not eliminate uncertainty. At some point, the remaining uncertainty must be evaluated not through more analysis but through judgment — through an honest assessment of whether the downside is survivable and the process is sound, regardless of what the outcome turns out to be. I told him this directly. He made the acquisition. It performed. More importantly, the next acquisition required less deliberation, because the process had been understood rather than just observed.

As others grew more capable, my responsibility shifted. It became less about providing answers and more about reinforcing standards — and about the particular discipline of allowing people to carry weight, make mistakes, and learn without being rescued from every consequence.

That discipline is harder than it sounds. The instinct when someone you have invested in makes a mistake is to correct it quickly — to step in, provide the answer, smooth the difficulty. That instinct is not wrong in every circumstance. In the early stages of development, direct correction is appropriate. But at a certain point, allowing someone to navigate difficulty without rescue is not abandonment. It is the condition under which genuine competence develops.

A property manager I had worked with for several years encountered a significant resident relations situation that she had not dealt with before — a dispute that had legal dimensions, required careful documentation, and demanded communication with the resident that was both firm and fair. My instinct was to take it over. I had dealt with similar situations before and could have resolved it faster and more confidently than she could at that stage.

I did not take it over. I made myself available for consultation, answered the specific questions she brought to me, and let her manage the situation. It took longer than it would have taken me. The resolution she arrived at was not identical to what I would have done, though it was sound. What she developed in the process — the confidence that she could handle a situation of that complexity, the specific judgment that comes from having navigated something difficult rather than watched someone else navigate it — could not have been developed any other way.

Accountability without abandonment means remaining present without removing the weight. It means being reachable without being indispensable. The distinction is not always comfortable to maintain, but it is the condition under which stewardship actually multiplies rather than simply concentrates.

Multiplication is not scale for its own sake. It is the transfer of judgment, values, and discipline so that responsibility can be carried well by others — in your presence and, eventually, without it.

I know the transfer has occurred when I receive a report on a decision that was made correctly, that I was not consulted on, and that reflects the same standards and the same care that I would have applied. Not a copy of what I would have decided — people with good judgment do not all arrive at identical conclusions — but a decision that was made through a process I recognize and that accounts honestly for the interests of the people affected by it.

Those moments are quiet. There is no announcement that accompanies them. The deal closes, the situation is resolved, the resident issue is handled — and somewhere in the documentation of what happened is evidence that the judgment required to handle it well has been transferred. That transfer is the work. Everything else is the context in which the work occurs.

I never sought to build dependence. My aim was always continuity — operations, relationships, and judgment that would function and compound beyond my direct involvement. True partnership and effective mentorship succeed only when others can operate responsibly without you present. That standard is harder to meet than it sounds, and it takes longer than most leaders are comfortable waiting for. But it is the only standard that produces something durable.

Leadership ultimately reveals itself not in what we build, but in what continues after we are gone.

LESSON

Partnership multiplies capacity. Mentorship multiplies judgment.

Sustainable growth depends on aligning character, process, and accountability.

CHAPTER 10

Legacy and the Long View

> *Legacy is shaped by decisions made long before their results appear.*

The story told in these chapters begins with a ten-year-old standing at a stranger's door at dinner hour, holding a receipt book, asking to be paid for newspapers already delivered. It ends — if it can be said to end — with a portfolio marked ten years old, investors whose capital had compounded through a pandemic and a correction and a recovery, and a team capable of operating responsibly in the absence of constant direction.

The distance between those two points was not traveled quickly. It was traveled through the accumulation of decisions — most of them small, many of them unremarkable in the moment, a few of them consequential in ways that only became visible years after they were made. What made the distance traversable was not exceptional talent or exceptional circumstances. It was a framework for carrying responsibility that was built gradually, tested repeatedly, and refined through the particular education that mistakes provide when they are examined honestly.

Legacy is not something pursued at the end of a career. It is formed by how decisions are made long before outcomes are known. Markets move in cycles. Businesses rise and fall. People, however, live in decades. When decisions are framed with a long view, urgency gives way to patience, and short-term pressure loses its grip. What appears conservative in the moment often proves resilient over time.

Growth without perspective creates fragility.

Growth with patience creates something that lasts.

Expansion that outruns judgment eventually demands compromise. I measure success less by acceleration and more by durability. The question is not how fast something can grow, but how well it holds together under strain.

In 2025 we marked ten years of ownership and management of three multifamily properties. During that decade the assets endured several distinct cycles: the stable growth period from 2015 to 2019, the extreme volatility of COVID-19 from 2020 to 2022, the supply-driven correction from 2023 to 2025. Over those ten years, our investors received triple-digit returns on their investments.

That summary is accurate and it is insufficient. The number does not describe what a decade of stewardship actually required. The cycles do not describe what it felt like to navigate them. The principles established in the prior chapters of this book were not proven in favorable conditions — they were proven in the ones that were not.

The COVID period was the most consequential test the portfolio encountered. In March and April of 2020, the operating assumptions underlying every multifamily property in the country became uncertain simultaneously. Residents lost income without warning. The regulatory environment changed within weeks in ways that affected lease enforcement, eviction timelines, and the legal structure of the landlord-resident relationship. Supply chains for maintenance and renovation materials became unreliable. The timeline for anything that required contractors or permitting extended in ways no underwriting model had or could have accounted for.

The decision made at the beginning of that period was to prioritize residents over revenue. That decision required explanation to investors, because its short-term effect on collections was visible and its long-term effect on retention and reputation was not yet demonstrable. The investor communications during that period were among the most difficult I have written — honest about what was unknown, clear about what had been decided and why, and specific about the range of outcomes the portfolio was likely to navigate depending on how conditions evolved.

Several investors, on receiving those communications, asked whether they should be concerned. My answer was consistent: concern about outcomes is reasonable, confidence about process is warranted. The properties were managed by a team that had been built for exactly this kind of pressure. The capital structure was conservative enough to absorb a period of reduced collections without requiring decisions that would damage the resident relationships the portfolio depended on for long-term performance. The liquidity position that had felt cautious in 2019 felt prudent in 2020.

Residents who experienced a management team that communicated honestly, that worked with them during a period of genuine hardship, and that prioritized their stability over short-term collection metrics did not leave when conditions improved. The retention through and immediately after the COVID period was stronger than the market average for comparable properties. That outcome was not accidental. It was the compounded result of how the portfolio had been operated for the five years before the crisis arrived.

The supply-driven correction from 2023 to 2025 required a different discipline — patience in the face of market softness that was structural rather than cyclical, and the restraint to avoid the pricing decisions that would have accelerated lease-up at the cost of resident quality and long-term stability. The conservative leverage structure established in the original acquisitions meant that carrying costs during that period were manageable without pressure to optimize for occupancy at any price. Patience, in that context, was not a virtue. It was a structural feature of how the portfolio had been built.

Ten years. Four cycles. Triple-digit returns. The number is accurate. What it represents is a decade of decisions made before outcomes were known, by a team that understood what it was responsible for and why.

The principle is the same whether managing millions of dollars or a seasonal small business.

When my wife Betty and I decided to start a snow-cone business, we approached it with the same long-term discipline that had shaped every other operational decision I had made. We researched thoroughly — visiting other operators, meeting and speaking directly with equipment suppliers, understanding the failure modes of the business before committing to its success modes. We purchased reliable equipment with backup parts rather than the cheapest option available, because we had learned many times over that the cost of equipment failure during peak demand is never limited to the repair cost. We installed our own water filtration system and ice maker to reduce dependence on external vendors. We stocked supplies locally to avoid the disruption that a delayed delivery produces during the hours when the demand is highest and the margin for error is lowest.

We also understood that longevity depends on trust — and that trust, in a neighborhood business, is built through consistent presence over time. On opening day each year, we gave away free snow cones so the neighborhood would know we were back for another season. That practice was not marketing. It was communication before comfort — showing up with value before we needed anything in return, making our presence known before we required the community's patronage to sustain it. The same principle that governed investor communication governed the opening day of a snow-cone stand. The scale was different. The logic was identical.

The business was not designed for a quick win. It was built for continuity — and continuity, in a seasonal business as in a long-term investment, is the measure of whether the discipline applied to building it was the right discipline.

Before investor or operator, I am a husband and father. No achievement offsets misalignment at home. Stewardship begins there.

That statement is easy to write and genuinely difficult to live. The pressure of managing a portfolio, raising capital, developing a team, and staying current with the markets that affect every decision I make is continuous and does not schedule itself around family dinners or school events or the ordinary, unhurried conversations that relationships require to stay healthy. The discipline of protecting family time is not natural in the environment that portfolio management creates. It is chosen, repeatedly, against the default pull of the work.

Betty has been a partner in the stewardship story in a way that this book cannot fully describe. She recognized potential before results — in the early years when the portfolio was being built and the returns were not yet visible, when the work was demanding more than the business was producing, and when the faith required to continue was, on some days, more hers than mine. Her discernment has served as a guardrail more times than I have counted. Her willingness to name what she observed — about my priorities, my pace, my tendency to let the work expand into spaces it should not occupy — was not always comfortable to receive, and was almost always correct.

The discipline to protect family time produced something that I did not fully anticipate: it modeled, for our children, the relationship between values and decisions in a way that no instruction could have replicated. Elizabeth, Aaron, and Derek grew up watching a father who worked hard and who also stopped. Who built things and who also came home. Who took responsibility seriously and who also took Sundays seriously. That observation — sustained across years, not demonstrated on a single occasion — is a form of stewardship that does not appear in any investor report or business plan, and whose returns compound in ways that are not financially measurable.

Success that erodes those foundations is not success — it is exchange. I have made that exchange in smaller ways at various points — a trip missed, an evening unavailable, a season when the work expanded beyond what I had committed to limiting it to. Those decisions had costs that I recognized at the time and that I would make differently with the judgment I have now. The goal is not perfection in this as in everything else. The goal is honest accounting, consistent direction, and the willingness to correct when the accounting reveals a drift that matters.

Legacy is not control. It is continuity.

True impact is measured by how well others operate when you are no longer present.

If systems fail without you, leadership has not been transferred.

If judgment cannot be replicated, responsibility has not been shared.

My goal has never been to build dependence. It has been to build capability — in people, in process, and in culture. When others succeed independently, stewardship has multiplied. When they make sound decisions without my involvement, continuity has been achieved. When the team navigates a difficult situation with the same care and the same principles that I would have applied, and does so without requiring my involvement, the work of stewardship has produced what it was designed to produce.

I have seen that happen. It does not happen quickly and it does not happen without the investment described in these chapters — without the hiring decisions that prioritized character, without the systems built for resilience rather than efficiency, without the mentorship that focused on process rather than outcomes, without the years of communication that modeled what honest accountability looks like in practice. But when it happens, it is unmistakable. And it is the only measure of legacy that I trust.

The long view requires humility. I do not assume I will always be right. I design decisions to remain sound even when conditions change. That humility creates space for learning, correction, and peace.

It also makes it possible to receive correction from others without defending against it. Several of the most consequential course corrections in my professional life came from people who were willing to tell me something I was not yet fully prepared to hear — Del Walmsley's insistence on cash flow before appreciation, Betty's observation about pace and priority, a trusted advisor's candid assessment of a deal structure that I had convinced myself was sound. In each case, the humility required was not the humility of self-deprecation. It was the humility of being genuinely open to the possibility that someone else's view of the situation was more accurate than my own.

That openness is not natural for someone whose professional identity is built on judgment. The instinct is to defend the judgment when it is questioned, particularly in front of others. The discipline is to examine the question before defending against it — to distinguish between challenges that reflect a misunderstanding and challenges that reflect a gap in your own analysis. The former can be corrected with explanation. The latter requires something more: the willingness to say that the assessment has changed and to act accordingly, without the performance of certainty that was never warranted.

Over time, the lessons described in these chapters distilled into a set of principles that guide every major decision I make. I refer to them simply as The Stewardship Code.

The Code did not arrive as a list. It arrived as experience — as the residue of decisions made well and decisions made poorly, of principles applied under pressure and principles that dissolved under pressure and had to be rebuilt. Each item in the Code can be traced to a specific period, a specific decision, a specific consequence that made the principle visible in a way that abstraction never could. The carpenter who could not meet a deadline. The bus operation that collapsed under conditions it had not been designed to survive. The renovation that revealed what conservative underwriting actually means when the walls are opened. The investor communication that confirmed what honesty produces when it precedes rather than follows a problem.

I offer the Code not as a formula for success but as an honest account of what stewardship has required across the span of experience described in these pages. The principles will not produce identical outcomes in different hands and different circumstances. But they will produce the same orientation — toward protection before performance, toward alignment before urgency, toward the kind of judgment that survives not just favorable conditions but the ones that test everything you have built.

Legacy is lived forward. It is expressed through decisions that honor people, principles, and patience. When judgment is exercised consistently over time, outcomes endure beyond the moment — and responsibility is carried well into the future.

If my children and those who work alongside me carry these principles further than I have, then the work of stewardship will have succeeded — not because the principles are mine, but because they are true, and because they will encounter circumstances I cannot anticipate and produce outcomes I will not be present to see. That is what stewardship means when it is complete: the transfer of judgment that continues past the point of your own involvement.

I wrote this book because I believe the lessons it contains are worth passing on — not because they are exceptional, but because they are rare in the places where they are most needed. In environments that reward speed, scale, and certainty, the discipline of stewardship is perpetually under pressure. The principles described here are not natural defaults. They are chosen positions, maintained against the grain of the environments in which most consequential decisions are made. They require practice, not just conviction. They require systems, not just intentions. And they require the humility to accept that the work of building them is never finished — only continued.

That continuity — not control — is the legacy I hope to leave behind.

LESSON

Legacy is lived forward.

When decisions honor people, principles, and patience, outcomes endure beyond the moment.

The Stewardship Summary

Stewardship is not formed in a single moment. It develops gradually through responsibility, pressure, and judgment.

Each stage of life teaches a different discipline.

Childhood teaches responsibility.
Early work reveals that effort and accountability shape opportunity.

Adaptation teaches resilience.
When familiar assumptions disappear, survival requires learning quickly and adjusting without complaint.

Responsibility teaches judgment.
Competence may open doors, but only sound judgment sustains responsibility when pressure arrives.

Influence teaches integrity.
Words carry weight only when belief, actions, and outcomes remain aligned over time.

Faith teaches alignment.
Opportunity is no longer something to seize but something entrusted. Conviction governs restraint when momentum encourages speed.

Stewardship teaches discipline.
Capital, people, and trust must be protected before results appear.

Partnership teaches multiplication.
Capacity grows when character aligns and responsibility is shared.

Legacy teaches the long view.
Decisions made with patience and humility endure beyond the moment.

Stewardship is not measured by speed or scale.
It is measured by the consistency of judgment applied over time.

When responsibility is carried with discipline, integrity, and restraint, outcomes become durable—and leadership becomes transferable.

THE STEWARDSHIP CODE

1. **Stewardship is practiced before outcomes are known.**
   Decisions reveal character long before results confirm them.

2. **Capital is protected before it is grown.**
   Downside matters more than acceleration.

3. **Alignment precedes opportunity.**
   Partnership without shared values creates hidden risk.

4. **Competence earns trust; consistency sustains it.**
   Titles do not grant authority—reliability does.

5. **Speed amplifies mistakes.**
   Patience preserves judgment.

6. **Systems must survive stress.**
   If a process fails under pressure, it is not complete.

7. **Responsibility cannot be outsourced.**
   Delegation requires inspection.
   Authority requires accountability.

8. **Character is difficult to teach after adulthood.**
   Selection matters more than correction.

9. **Faith governs restraint, not certainty.**
   Conviction should slow decisions, not rush them.

10. **Legacy is continuity, not control.**
    Stewardship succeeds when others can operate without you.

The Stewardship Framework

1. **Responsibility Before Opportunity**
   Opportunity rarely appears before responsibility is proven. Carry small responsibilities faithfully before seeking larger ones.

2. **Judgment Before Speed**
   Momentum rewards action, but stewardship requires discernment. Not every opportunity deserves pursuit.

3. **Protection Before Optimism**
   Assume conditions will not unfold perfectly. Design decisions that survive delays, mistakes, and uncertainty.

4. **Liquidity Before Expansion**
   Cash reserves are not idle capital. They create time, and time allows sound judgment.

5. **Systems Before Heroics**
   Organizations that depend on exceptional individuals are fragile. Durable outcomes require systems that function without heroics.

6. **Transparency Before Comfort**
   Bad news improves with early communication. Trust compounds when honesty precedes convenience.

7. **Alignment Before Outcome**
   When conviction governs decisions, outcomes can be accepted without panic and corrected without excuse.

8. **Continuity Before Recognition**
   Leadership succeeds when others can operate responsibly without your presence.

Practicing Stewardship in Daily Decisions

Stewardship rarely appears dramatic. It is practiced in small decisions repeated over time.

Some questions I return to regularly include:

1. **What responsibility has been entrusted to me in this moment?**
   Before pursuing opportunity, recognize what has already been entrusted.

2. **What could go wrong, and who would carry the cost?**
   Sound decisions begin with honest consideration of downside risk.

3. **Does this opportunity require speed or judgment?**
   Momentum often encourages action. Stewardship asks whether action is wise.

4. **Are people protected if assumptions fail?**
   Responsible leadership ensures others are not exposed to avoidable risk.

5. **Would I make the same decision if recognition were impossible?**
   Stewardship is practiced even when outcomes remain unseen.

6. **Will this decision still make sense years from now?**
   The long view often reveals what short-term pressure obscures.

EPILOGUE

Stewardship rarely appears dramatic in the moment.

It reveals itself slowly through decisions repeated over time.

Responsibility accepted early forms judgment later.

Judgment practiced consistently builds trust.

Trust carried faithfully multiplies through others.

None of this happens quickly.

The work of stewardship is quiet. It happens in preparation, in restraint, and in choices made when no one is watching. It is rarely rewarded immediately, but its effects compound long after the decision has been made.

I no longer view success as something owned.

Opportunity is entrusted. Responsibility is carried.

Over time, the question that matters most is not how much has been built, but how well it endures when you are no longer present.

Legacy is not something pursued at the end of life.

It is formed every day in the way responsibility is carried forward.

Looking back, I sometimes think about the receipt books my father handed me when I was ten years old.

At the time, I believed I was simply earning a computer.

Only later did I realize he was teaching something far more important: responsibility must be carried before rewards appear.

In many ways, the lessons of stewardship began there.

I no longer see the events of my life as accomplishments to be claimed.

Opportunities appeared, responsibilities followed, and decisions had to be carried with care. Some outcomes were favorable. Others required correction. All of them required judgment.

In the end, the goal was never ownership. It was stewardship.

If anything meaningful has been built, it is because the opportunities entrusted to me were carried with patience, discipline, and faith.

The work was never to conquer life, but to steward it faithfully.

Acknowledgments

This book reflects the influence of many people who invested time, wisdom, and patience into my life—often without knowing the full impact of their guidance.

I am grateful to Del Walmsley and the Lifestyles Unlimited community for providing education, mentoring, structure, and accountability at a critical time. The lessons learned there reshaped how I understood real estate, partnership, and stewardship — particularly Del's three rules: don't lose money, it has to cash flow, and the counterintuitive reminder that you can't get rich slow.

I thank Tom Ziglar for his friendship, counsel, and example. His steady leadership and commitment to faith-centered values reinforced principles that endure far beyond business. I am equally thankful to Julie and Cindy Ziglar for their encouragement and support.

I am grateful to John C. Maxwell for his leadership teachings, which helped me understand responsibility as the stewardship of influence exercised with humility.

I appreciate Bob Beaudine for timely reminders about the importance of relationships and purpose, and for reinforcing the value of surrounding oneself with the right people.

I am grateful for the teachings and the sage counsel of Dr. Robert A. Rohm and Mrs. April Dawn Rohm. Their influence deepened my understanding of human behavior and communication, and the many conversations I shared with them sharpened my perspective on marriage and family relationships.

I am deeply grateful for the pastors of Plano Chinese Alliance Church over the past thirty-five years. Their introduction to the Gospel, years of patient pursuit, and consistent nurturing laid the foundation of my faith. Without their guidance, I would not know Jesus Christ as my Savior and would remain, as Zig Ziglar often warned, a "wandering generality."

This work is not possible without the dedicated and resourceful team at ABCDE Realty Management and Genie Construction. Their acceptance of delegated responsibilities gave me the time and space to think and write. They are the unsung heroes behind the scenes.

Finally, I am thankful to my wife for her unwavering prayer, discernment, and support, and to my family for their patience as this journey unfolded.

Each contribution represented here is part of the stewardship described in these pages.

About the Author

Charles Ho is an entrepreneur, investor, and mentor whose work spans real estate, small business ownership, and operational leadership. Born in Taiwan, he immigrated to the United States as a teenager and learned early that responsibility, discipline, and adaptability were essential to survival and growth.

Over several decades, Charles built and stewarded businesses across multiple industries, including information technology, automotive services, food and beverage operations, and real estate investing. His experience includes acquisitions, operations, financing, investor relations, and property management, with a consistent focus on downside protection, systems design, and long-term sustainability.

Charles began building a real estate portfolio in 1996 through self-service car washes. In 2011, his focus expanded to single-family and multifamily assets, serving as a lead investor, partner, and mentor. He has worked directly with hundreds of investors and families, emphasizing stewardship, risk management, and long-term alignment over short-term performance.

He approaches investing and leadership through the lens of stewardship. His decisions are guided by faith, restraint, and a commitment to protecting people and capital before pursuing growth. He values alignment over urgency and character over convenience, believing that durable outcomes result from disciplined judgment applied consistently over time.

Charles is a Ziglar Certified Coach and has served as a multifamily mentor with Lifestyles Unlimited, guiding new and experienced investors through acquisitions, operations, and decision-making under pressure. In addition to his business activities, he has spent years mentoring individuals and families seeking clarity around leadership, investing, and personal responsibility.

Charles maintains the National Apartment Association's CAPS and CAMT credentials.

Charles is a Texas-licensed portable fire extinguisher inspector.

Charles lives in Texas with his wife and family. Together, they prioritize faith, family, and long-term stewardship in both life and business.

www.ingramcontent.com/pod-product-compliance
Lightning Source LLC
LaVergne TN
LVHW010933110826

845149LV00013B/2577

9781972345047